PAINTINGS:

How to Look at Great Art

by Ann Campbell

FRANKLIN WATTS

New York/London

To Peter Paul Luce, whose clarity of thought
and word, plus enduring patience, was indispensable.

The color photographs in this book, as well as the black and white illustrations on pages 20, 35, and 95 (top), are reproduced through the courtesy of Grolier Incorporated. All other black and white photographs, with the exception of those on pages 23, 81, and 89 (and those listed above) are by Jonathan Baird.

PRODUCED BY GEORGE RAINBIRD LTD, LONDON

SBN 531-01867-9

Contents

Introduction

It is easy to look and never see. But if you know what to look for you will see new things, not just in paintings but all around you.

The purpose of this book is to show you what to look for in paintings, and in looking at them again and again, to find new enjoyment.

It is important to start at the beginning of this book, for you will find that the principles and concepts of how to look at a painting unfold simply and naturally. However, if you jump in at random you may find it confusing.

While the paintings are presented chronologically, the emphasis is on the paintings themselves, rather than on history. Too often a work of art is placed in a period with a historical handle, such as the Renaissance, baroque, classic, or rococo, but the paintings themselves are never really looked at. In this book these historical handles have been purposely left out. For example, if you look at the photograph on the opposite page and read: "Skunk Cabbage—a plant with thick roots, wide leaves, and disagreeable smell," you will not want to look at the cabbage itself. But if you get down on your knees and study it (holding your breath), you will find a pattern of delicate lines, curling shapes, velvety shadows, and fresh beauty.

There are times, however, when history does dictate what the artist paints, and how he paints it. For this reason a historical list has been included in the back of the book, to let the artist and his work slip quietly into history.

What Do You See When You Look?

Start to look at paintings and you will see your own world with fresh eyes.

What did you see when you were out walking today? Did you look down at the cracks in the sidewalk? Sometimes they look like an elephant or a tiger, sometimes they make a wonderful jagging pattern.

Did you ever notice the shadow of an empty trash basket on the street? It makes a beautiful crisscross pattern. Did you ever look at the design on the top of a fire hydrant, or the wonderful colors in the tail of a bird? Did you ever go to the zoo and look at the polar bear's cage, or take a walk in the woods and look at the skunk cabbage? Everywhere you look you will see patterns of lines and shapes. Patterns of lines and shapes are called designs.

There are so many things you should look at again. Things you missed when you first looked. And so it is with paintings. You must look at them not just once, but many times. For paintings tell you things and make you feel things: they can make you laugh or cry, be angry, happy, or afraid. They can even make a loud noise—or so it seems. But most paintings are like a tune that gets better as you keep on humming it.

Should a Painting Look Like a Photograph?

Let us say that I took a photograph of you, as you are right this minute. And it looks just like you. Let us also say that I painted a picture of you. You told me what you would like to be someday— perhaps a fireman, an airplane pilot, or a fashion designer. You told me about the play you were in, the fish you caught in the pond in the park, your favorite book, the cake you like best to eat, and of course, your dog Chuffy. And so I put all these things into the picture of you.

Now, which shows the real you?—the photograph or the painting? The painting, of course, because it tells all about you, while the photograph caught only a single second that was you.

So a painting does not have to look like a photograph to be good, but it must tell you something and make you feel something.

Bison: from the Lascaux Caves, about 12,000 B.C.

Here is a painting of running bison found on the walls of a cave, painted by cavemen in 12,000 B.C. It is one of the earliest known paintings. The bison are afraid and running, in two directions, for the hunters are probably chasing them with arrows or spears. You can see their mouths bellowing and imagine that their eyes are wide with fear. It is thought that the paintings on the wall were intended to give the hunters a special magic in hunting. This painting tells you about the bison running, but it also tells you about their fear.

Bison: from the Lascaux Caves, about 12,000 B.C. Dordogne, France.
Photo courtesy of Life Magazine, Time-Life Inc.

Fowling in the Marshes. Copy of a fresco from the tomb of Nakht, about 1500 B.C.

This Egyptian painting also tells about a hunt. A nobleman (Nakht, shown twice) stands in his small boat in the marshes and tries to catch ducks and geese by flinging a boomerang into the air. As the birds are caught they are stuffed into a bag by Nakht's son (also shown twice), standing in the bow of the boat. Nahkt is the largest figure in the painting for he is the most important. The slaves (at the extreme right and left) are the smallest and least important. But why are the feet and heads of all the figures turned to the side, while their shoulders face the front?No one really knows why, but for more than three thousand years it was the custom of Egyptian artists to always paint figures in this way.

Do you feel afraid for the birds? Probably not, for this is a gay, busy story, rather like the one about fishing in the pond.

Patterns of Lines and Shapes

What is this a picture of? Can you believe it is just the shadow of an empty trash basket on the sidewalk? The crisscross lines repeat over and over to form a pattern.

Look at the page opposite, showing the Egyptian hunting scene. Can you find any patterns? Look at the way the artist made a pattern of lines and shapes in the marsh across the back of the painting. It is a beautiful pattern of green and yellow papyrus flowers and buds. The lines and flower shapes repeat over and over.

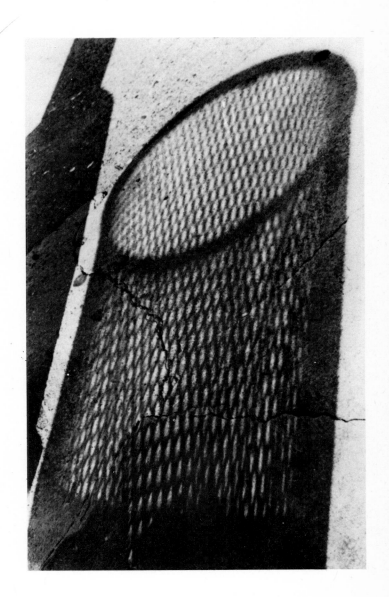

Greek Vase: "Harnessing a Chariot," about 510 B.C.

"Harnessing a Chariot" was painted on a Greek vase around 510 B.C. The painting tells you that three men and the charioteer are harnessing the horses to the chariot. But how many horses are there? Count the back and front legs of the horse in front, and you will see that there are really two horses. The repeating lines of their legs make a pattern of lines. Do they remind you of the repeating lines in the trash-basket shadow? See how the third horse tosses his head, struggling to get free. Can you see that the folds of the white robe on the charioteer also make a pattern of straight lines? Now look below. Two men on horseback are flinging spears at a charging wild boar. The black shapes of the men, horses, and boar make a zigzagging pattern of black shapes across the bottom of the vase.

Greek vase: Harnessing a Chariot, about 510 B.C. *London, British Museum*

Theodora and Her Courtiers (detail), mid-sixth century

This mosaic on the walls of the Church of S. Vitale tells you that the Empress Theodora, who is presenting a jeweled chalice to the church, was a Christian and wanted all her people to be Christians as well. Notice the patterns. On the robes of the two ladies on the right are patterns of circles, flowers, and fishes. The folds of all their robes fall in graceful patterns, some falling straight down, others repeating a curve. Look at the pattern of jewels on the crown and collar of the empress. Even the eyes and eyebrows in all of the faces form a pattern of curving lines, as do the long slender fingers. But although the eyes and brows form patterns of curving lines, the shape of each face is different, as is each mouth.

To make a mosaic the artist uses tiny pieces of colored stones instead of paint, pressing them into wet plaster or cement. Here the artist has drawn each figure with a dark line of stones, filling the spaces in between with lighter and brighter stones.

The inside walls of churches were often covered with paintings or mosaics showing Christ and the saints.

Theodora and Her Courtiers (detail), mid-sixth century. Mosaic. *Ra-venna, San Vitale*

CIMABUE
The Madonna Enthroned with Angels, about 1280

This painting has many patterns in it. But first let us see what the painting tells you. Mary, the mother of Jesus Christ, sits on the throne, holding the infant Christ Child in her lap. The angels, who are less important and smaller, stand one above the other, on each side. But why did Cimabue paint everyone looking so serious and sad? Probably because he knew that Christ would be crucified. Christ is making the sign of the blessing with his right hand, as if he were already grown up.

Can you find some patterns in the picture? Look at the patterns of lines on the brown throne. See how the folds of Mary's blue dress make a pattern of lines as they wrap around her, letting you sense her body underneath. The four angels make a pattern too. Even the gold halos make a pattern of flat circles running into each other at the top of the picture. While this painting tells you about the birth of Jesus Christ, it also tells you about his death. It is a sad picture.

CIMABUE   The Madonna Enthroned with Angels, about 1280. Tempera on panel. *Paris, Louvre*

SIMONE MARTINI
Guidoriccio da Fogliano, 1328

Can you find the many patterns in this painting? What a wonderful pattern of black diamonds, dots, and green flowers covers Guidoriccio's armor and that of his horse. The picket fence going around the castle and walled town, and the spears of the soldiers hiding behind it, also make a lively pattern. How proud Guidoriccio is, riding his prancing horse. His horse bares its teeth, its nostrils quiver in a pattern of curving lines, and its marvelous eye peeks out through the hole in the armor. When you look at Guidoriccio's round face and stomach you know that he loves to eat and drink in his castle in the distance. But how far away is the castle? The castle, the walled town, and the hills are painted like a backdrop in a play, and Guidoriccio rides in front of it like one of the actors in the play.

SIMONE MARTINI   Guidoriccio da Fogliano, 1328. Fresco. *Siena, Palazzo Pubblico*

SIMONE MARTINI   Guidoriccio da Fogliano (detail), 1328. Fresco. *Siena,*
Palazzo Pubblico

Composition Is Like a Road Map

The picture on the opposite page is a road map, put here to illustrate a point.

Why doesn't your eye wander outside of a painting when you are looking at it? It doesn't because the artist carefully plans to keep your eye in it. Every great painting has a plan behind it. This plan is called a composition. A composition is like a road map. It carries your eye in and around the painting, forcing it to come back to the most important thing in the painting, which is called a focal point.

Look at the road map. The roads weave all around, but the place most of them lead to is Little Rock, which in this map is the focal point. The same thing happens in a painting. The difference is that the artist uses lines, shapes, or color to get you where he wants you to go. Not all paintings have focal points. Sometimes the artist keeps your eye always on the move.

GIOTTO
Lamentation over Christ, about 1305–06

In this fresco, where does Giotto try to take your eye? Your eye keeps coming back to Mary, cradling in her arms the heavy head of the dead Christ, her son. If you start looking at the painting at the top right, your eye carries you down the tree and then slides swiftly down the diagonal cliff to the heads of Mary and Christ. This is the focal point. Can you see that their two halos join them together? If your eye comes in on the left, it leaps over the heads of the crowd to the weeping figure in dark green and drops quickly to Mary. Do you think the two squatting figures with their backs to you look like two tombstones, framing Mary and Christ? Can you find other roads into the painting? On the right, the eyes and arms of the two standing men lead your eye to the figure in purple leaning toward Christ. The man on the right is perhaps Joseph of Arimathea, who has come to bury Christ. Mary Magdalene holds Christ's feet, while Mary, the mother of James, holds his hands. (There were three Marys at the tomb.)

Giotto's figures are solid and seem modeled out of clay, with a strong line around them. The folds of their clothes are molded with dark shadows, letting you sense their bodies underneath. But their faces show real grief, while their bodies bend in real sorrow. These are very real people. Do you see that the whole scene is crowded into the front as if all the actors in the play had pushed themselves out in front of the curtain?

GIOTTO   Lamentation over Christ, about 1305–06. *Padua, Arena Chapel*

PAOLO UCCELLO
St. George and the Dragon, about 1460

Can you find the focal point of this painting? The focal point is the dragon's open mouth, dripping blood, and his terrible teeth. Draw a "road map," or composition, of the way the artist keeps your eye inside the painting. Look for patterns of lines and shapes in the lady's pink dress, in the carpet of flowers, and in the wicked dragon's tail. Look, too, at the round, solid, almost wooden horse of St. George's.

The mountains seem so far away in the distance. Do they look like the hills and rocks in Giotto's *Lamentation over Christ* or the mountains and castle in Simone Martini's painting of *Guidoriccio da Fogliano?* These mountains seem to go way back into space. How do you suppose Uccello knew how to achieve this effect?

PAOLO UCCELLO   St. George and the Dragon, about 1460. Oil on panel.
London, National Gallery

POL DE LIMBOURG

April, from the manuscript the *Très Riches Heures du Duc de Berri,* about 1415

Très Riches Heures du Duc de Berri is a calendar and each page illustrates one month in the year. In this page for April, four elegant lords and ladies are exchanging a ring. Your eye is drawn to where all their hands join. Then your eye moves to the two ladies picking flowers, and back along the garden wall to the lake where two men in boats are fishing. In the far background is the Duc de Berri's lovely castle, or château. Your eye is not permitted to rest for long, and again moves along the trees to the front or foreground. But there is something odd here. Not only does your eye want to keep moving about the picture, but you are looking at this painting with five sets of eyes. You are looking *down* into the courtyard on the right, but *up* at the tower next to it. You look *up* at the castle in the distance but *down* on the lake. You are on the same level with the lords and ladies. Have you ever thought of looking at the world with five sets of eyes?

Look, too, at the brilliant blues, rusty reds, golds, and greens and at the many beautiful patterns. Can you see Taurus the Bull and Aries the Ram, signs of the zodiac for April, in the heavens above? And the Sun Chariot being driven across the sky?

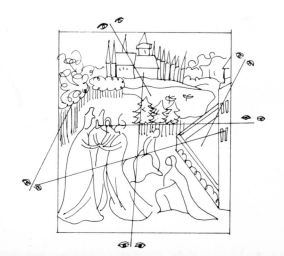

POL, HENNEQUIN, and HERMANN DE LIMBOURG   April, from the "Très Riches Heures du Duc de Berri," begun 1415. Vellum. *Chantilly, Musée Condé*

How Do You Paint Space?

If you put something in the foreground of your picture, how do you get something to go *behind* it? In the Egyptian painting, the marsh of papyrus flowers was hung like a backdrop across the back of the picture. In the *Madonna Enthroned*, Cimabue painted the angels above each other, trying to make them be *behind* each other. In the *Très Riches Heures*, the Limbourg brothers had you looking at things with five sets of eyes. But in *St. George and the Dragon*, the mountains really do look realistic and far away. How did Uccello do it?

Have you ever noticed that a car speeding down the highway seems to get smaller the farther away it moves? In the fifteenth century in Italy, artists discovered that by using mathematics they could figure out just how much smaller things seem to get as they go into space. This is called perspective.

On the opposite page is a perspective drawing. The double line is the horizon line. The horizon line is at your eye level. Along the horizon line is a point, called the vanishing point. Any line drawn from any point *above* the horizon line comes *down* to the vanishing point. Any line drawn from *below* the horizon comes *up* to the vanishing point. As the lines go back to the vanishing point, they meet, and the sizes of buildings, people, and things are measured by these lines, as they move back into space. (Note that a perpendicular line is always perpendicular no matter where it is in space.) In this diagram the vanishing point is in the center of the horizon line, but the artist can put it anywhere he chooses along this line. In the same way, the artist can put the horizon line as high or as low as he chooses, but once he decides, he must follow the rest of the rules.

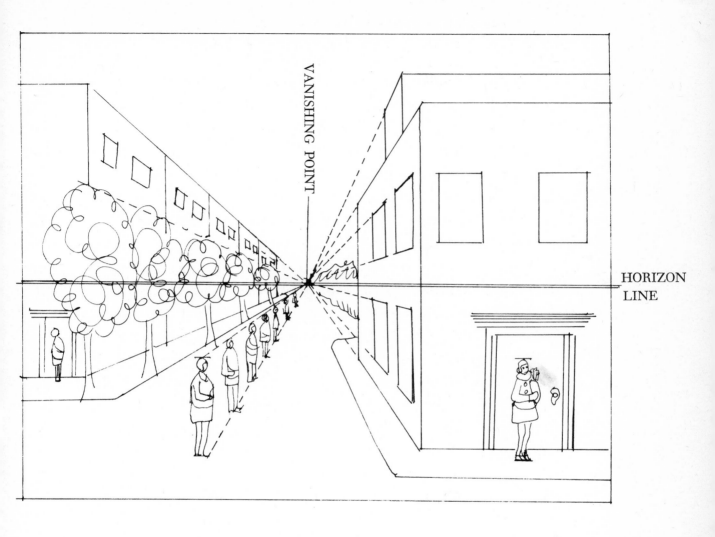

VANISHING POINT

HORIZON
LINE

PERUGINO

Christ Giving the Keys of the Church to St. Peter, about 1482

Look at this painting. Do the lines on the plaza remind you of the lines in the perspective drawing on the page before? Study the diagram under the painting. Can you find the horizon line and vanishing point in this painting? The vanishing point is in the center of the door of the domed church. It is also directly above the big key that Christ is giving to St. Peter and it draws your eye to that spot. The largest figures are in the foreground. Notice that the two lines drawn from the head and feet of the man in the left foreground to the vanishing point tell the artist how large to make the people standing in the middle ground and in the background. The buildings and feathery trees are in the background, with the mountains far away in the distance. You can even see some tiny people standing by the far wall on the left. Maybe the artist was more interested in painting perfect perspective than he was in telling us the story of Christ giving St. Peter the keys to the church. What do you think?

PERUGINO   Christ Giving the Keys of the Church to St. Peter, about
1482. Fresco. *Rome, Vatican, Sistine Chapel*

VANISHING POINT

HORIZON
LINE

RAPHAEL
The School of Athens (detail), 1509–12

Raphael has also put the vanishing point in the center of the horizon line. It comes just behind the heads of Socrates and Plato, the Greek philosophers, who stand under the dark archway. Study the diagram to see how Raphael used arches and rectangles to form a geometric composition, or "road map," even before he added his figures. The painting is planned from the center out. The figures are placed in groups on either side of the center, some sitting, standing, talking, or thinking. Each group might in itself be a painting. The man lying on the steps connects the groups and carries your eye back to Socrates and Plato, who are the focal point and are at the vanishing point. Can you see how the lines of perspective determine the sizes of the figures as they go back into space? But how solid the figures are. They look very lifelike, don't you think? Their bodies are modeled as if out of huge chunks of clay, while their clothes drape around them, letting you sense their powerful muscles underneath. Raphael used strong dark shadows to model the figures, and these add to the life and movement of this carefully planned painting.

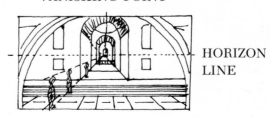

VANISHING POINT

HORIZON LINE

RAPHAEL   The School of Athens, 1509–12. Fresco. *Rome, Vatican, Stanza della Segnatura*

RAPHAEL   The School of Athens (detail), 1509–12.

Fog, or Sfumato

This is a photograph of a bridge looming out of the fog. What has happened to the sharp edges of the bridge in the distance? The fog and haze have blurred the hard outlines. Turn back to the Perugino painting, *Christ Giving the Keys of the Church to St. Peter,* and look at the feathery trees in the far background. If you look carefully you can see individual leaves. Could you see individual leaves if it were foggy? Certainly not; all you would see would be soft shapes that resembled trees.

LEONARDO DA VINCI   The Virgin and Child with St. Anne (detail), about
1516. Oil on panel. *Paris, Louvre*

LEONARDO DA VINCI
The Virgin and Child with St. Anne (detail), 1516

Look at this picture of the Virgin Mary with the Christ Child and St. Anne and see how different it is from Cimabue's *Madonna Enthroned*. Mary is shown as a very soft and warm mother and Jesus as a chubby, playful child. St. Anne was the mother of Mary, and to show this Leonardo has Mary sitting on her lap as Mary reaches out for the baby. (The lamb should remind you of John the Baptist.)

What makes this such a soft and warm and wonderful painting? Remember the bridge in the fog? Leonardo has painted the three figures as if they were surrounded by mist and haze. He has blurred the sharp edges, half-hidden the figures in shadows and touched their faces with warm light. Study, too, the hills and mountains in the distance. It is as if the sun had suddenly come through the rain clouds, bathing everything in a hazy blue light. There are no sharp outlines anywhere. The colors are bright in the foreground, greens and browns in the middle ground, and blue in the far background.

Now·look at the composition (the actual painting is much larger). The three figures form a large triangle. Inside the triangle, the arms, legs, bodies, and heads move your eye in a curving rhythm to the focal point, which is the head of the baby Jesus.

Touching Textures

Pretend that you are touching some of the actual things in the photograph on the opposite page. How would they feel to your fingers? How warm and furry the fur would feel, but how prickly the brush with the wooden handle. How smooth and slippery the glass decanter would feel, but how rough and scratchy the sandpaper and the rock. The candlestick would feel cold and hard, but the piece of flannel in the foreground would feel gently soft and warm.

Now, see how the light strikes each one of these things or textures. Very gently the light touches some of the fine hairs of the fur, while the shadows are soft and deep. But the light is sharp and the shadows hard on the bristly brush. On the glass decanter the light reflects itself like a mirror, while it catches on each of the tiny sand particles of the sandpaper and the rough bumps of the rock. The light bounces off the rounded and decorated parts of the brass candlestick, while it is absorbed on the piece of flannel and seems to go inside it.

Look around and touch things or textures near you. Touch your chair, the table, the floor or rug, your dress or pants, your notebook. Touch, too, the cold steel tip of your pencil and then the crumbly eraser. How does the light strike each of the textures or things that you touched?

JAN VAN EYCK
Portrait of Giovanni Arnolfini and His Wife, 1434

This painting tells about the marriage of Giovanni Arnolfini and his wife. Van Eyck has signed his own name on the wall behind, as a witness, saying, "Jan Van Eyck was here."

See, Arnolfini is holding his wife's hand. The little brown dog is a symbol of faithfulness, while the two pairs of slippers tell you that Arnolfini and his wife hope to love and respect each other.

How many different things or textures can you find to touch in this painting? Your fingers long to feel the fur of his robe, the smooth oranges at the window, the hairy dog, the hard wooden floor, the richly colored oriental rug, the brass chandelier, and so on. Look at the mirror on the wall behind the couple. Can you see how their backs and the whole room are reflected in the curved mirror?

Van Eyck painted thin layers of color (in oil paints) one on top of the other, as if they were layers of colored glass. The colors shine through from underneath, giving his paintings a special glow of rich color.

How did Van Eyck paint space? Can you see the lines of perspective on the floor? They are not exact. Do you think Van Eyck was more interested in light and textures than in space?

JAN VAN EYCK   Portrait of Giovanni Arnolfini and His Wife, 1434. Oil
on panel. *London, National Gallery*

HANS HOLBEIN THE YOUNGER
Portrait of Georg Gisze, 1532

How many different textures can you find to touch in this portrait of Georg Gisze? How does the light strike them? The light is reflected off the shiny pink satin sleeves, but it is absorbed by (or goes into) the black wool coat and cap.

Holbein has painted into the picture the tools of this man's trade, and there are many different textures here. Can you tell what this man does? Look at the slim scale on the left for measuring gold coins, the red sealing wax on the silk ribbons for important papers, the carefully written bills on paper, the string hanging from the patterned brass ball for wrapping packages, the leather file, the steel scissors on the table for cutting the string, quill pens, the inkwell, the gold stamp box, and of course, gold coins in the round pewter box. His accounting books are on the top shelves of the wood-paneled office. Here is another clue. Look at the richly patterned Oriental rug, from Persia, covering his table, and the delicate glass vase with the pink flowers, probably from Italy. You've guessed it. Georg Gisze was a successful merchant, and he looks out at you with his sharp eyes, probably wondering if you can pay your bill.

HANS HOLBEIN THE YOUNGER Portrait of Georg Gisze, 1532. Oil on panel. *West Berlin, Staatliche Museen*

How Do You Paint Movement and Energy?

Did you know that your own body can tell you lots of things about a painting? Which has the most movement and energy?—you standing still or you dancing about? You sitting in a chair or you doing somersaults? You lying flat on the floor or you running the 100-yard dash? Look at the page opposite for the lines and movements you make when you dance about, when you do somersaults, or when you run the 100-yard dash. But now look at the stillness of the lines when you are still.

It is the same in painting. The dancing lines and shapes, the curving rhythms, and the zooming diagonals give the greatest amount of movement and energy to a painting.

And of course, the opposite is true too. If you want a peaceful, quiet painting you should use horizontal and vertical lines or shapes. See what your body tells you about the paintings on the next few pages.

Movement

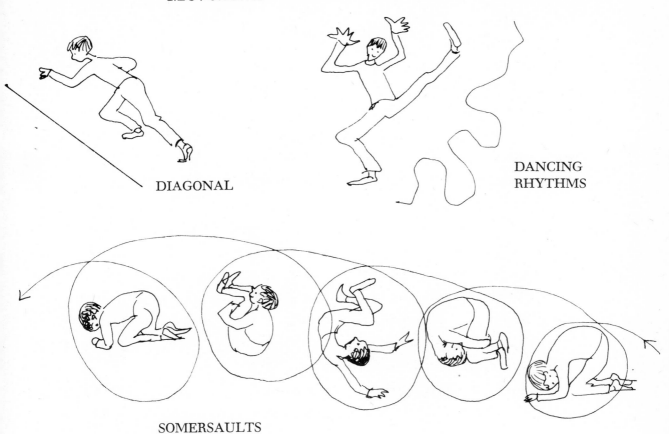

DIAGONAL

DANCING
RHYTHMS

SOMERSAULTS

Stillness

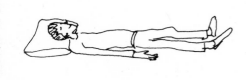

HORIZONTAL

VERTICAL

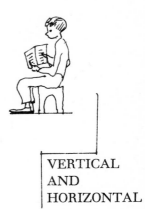

VERTICAL
AND
HORIZONTAL

PIETER BRUEGEL THE ELDER
The Peasant Wedding (detail), about 1568

Everyone is eating and drinking at this noisy peasant wedding. How has Bruegel put so much movement, energy, and noise into this painting? He has used diagonal shapes, dancing lines and curving rhythms. Your eye is quickly drawn into the painting and moves to the diagonals of the table, bench, and arms of the man reaching for the pies. It is carried back in and around the painting, somersaulting over heads and bodies of guests and bagpipers, bouncing over bowls, cups and round pies. Then your eye stops at the round-faced bride, who is the focal point. Can you see her, framed by a green blanket, sitting under a red and white crown? Her new husband in a green hat sits across from her shouting for more wine. Do you think he is handsome?

Look, a small child sits all alone in the corner stuffing a pie into her mouth with her fingers.

How many different textures can you find? Wood, piecrust, straw, clay pots, brass, wool, and linen. But what keeps this painting from being too busy? Bruegel has fuzzed the outlines of each figure, fusing them into one crowd—a noisy, merry crowd. He makes you hear the whine of the bagpipes, the clanking of tin cups, laughter, and even the small noise of the child licking her fingers.

PIETER BRUEGEL THE ELDER   The Peasant Wedding (detail), about
1568. Oil on panel. *Vienna, Kunsthistorisches Museum*

MICHELANGELO

The Delphic Sibyl (detail from the Sistine Chapel ceiling), 1508–12

The Delphic Sibyl is one of the panels in the huge (45 feet by 128 feet) fresco painted on the ceiling of the Sistine Chapel. Michelangelo was not only a painter but a sculptor and architect as well. Can you find some rhythmic curves, diagonals, and dancing lines in this painting? Follow the powerful curves of the Sibyl's cloak, the swirling folds of her skirt, the huge curve of her knee and foot, the strong curving arm that holds the scroll, the diagonal right arm with her big curled hand. The Delphic Sibyl is so overpowering that she seems carved out of stone, rather than painted, don't you think? Even the colors have an earthlike quality. Can you see that she bursts right out of the niche in which she sits? Compare this painting with Leonardo's *Virgin and Child with St. Anne* on page 38. Is there any softness or sfumato in this painting? No. The shadows with the strong outline around the forms harden her, rather than soften her.

When Bruegel used movement there was noise and clatter, but here there is no noise. With her twisted body, the Sibyl seems to be holding back some great energy, movement, and outcry. Have you ever watched a baseball pitcher wind up, gathering and tightening his strength like a coiled spring before he fires the pitch? It is this kind of power the Delphic Sibyl is holding back.

MICHELANGELO   The Delphic Sybil (detail from ceiling), 1508–12.
Fresco. *Rome, Vatican, Sistine Chapel*

EL GRECO
The Burial of Count Orgaz, 1586–88

Can you follow the whirling shapes and curving rhythms in this painting? St. Stephen on the right, and St. Augustine, left, are lifting the dead body of the count, heavy in his armor, while his friends look sadly on. The small boy on the left peers out at you, inviting you to look at the miracle of the count going to heaven. The priest at the right is celebrating the funeral mass for the friends.

The picture is in three parts: above, heaven; the miracle in the center; and the mass for the count at the bottom. You can see St. Peter with the keys to the gates of heaven, the angels with their harps, Mary, and the tiny cherubs flying about. The whole painting seems to whirl upward like a flame, ending with Jesus Christ in a white robe at the very top.

How firm and solid the bottom, or earthly, half of the painting is. The heavy black clothes of the mourners and the heavy brocaded robes of the bishops seem to hold it down. By contrast, in the heavens, the colors have a lightness and eerie shimmer, and the folds of the clothes swirl upward in gusts of unseen winds. The whole painting makes you feel a tremendous religious energy.

EL GRECO   The Burial of Count Orgaz, 1586–88. Oil on canvas. *Toledo, S. Tomé*

SIR PETER PAUL RUBENS
The Landing of Maria de' Medici at Marseilles, about 1625

Maria de' Medici, queen of France, arrives at Marseilles. She stands on the deck of her ship, in front of the mast, high above eye level, surrounded by her court and ladies-in-waiting. A cloaked nobleman, leaning diagonally toward her, invites her to step under the canopy, which is held up by servants, while an angel flies diagonally above Maria, tooting on two trumpets at once. The painting tells the legendary story of Maria de' Medici's arrival in France. The nymphs in the foreground are mythological creatures. Can you see one nymph pulling on the line from the ship, while another makes it fast to the piling? Poseidon himself, the king of the sea in mythology, is giving orders. The diagonal pull and push of the nymphs' arms attract your eye. Their bodies twist and water swirls about their fishtails. Flags, clothes, and clouds somersault in never-ending curves and diagonals. The brush-strokes themselves have movement and excitement, and they soften any harsh outlines around the figures.

But what about textures? There is everything here: clouds, air, mist, water, marble, wood, satin, silk, velvet brocade, armor, and lots of rosy, fleshy skin.

Do you realize that you are standing in the water with the nymphs, looking up at Maria de' Medici?

SIR PETER PAUL RUBENS The Landing of Maria de' Medici at Marseilles, about 1625. Oil on canvas. *Paris, Louvre*

Chiaroscuro, or Light and Shadow

Look at the photograph on the right. Two rock and roll singers are singing into a microphone while strumming frantically on their guitars. The air seems electric and deafening as the amplifiers blast the sounds. The spotlight picks up their kinetic hands on the strings; it lights up the cable of the microphone and touches their shouting faces. The rest of them is swallowed up by the darkness. You can almost hear the screaming audience go wild.

When an artist creates this same theatrical effect with paint, it is called *chiaroscuro* (key-ar-os-CUR-ro). Chiaroscuro is an Italian word that means light and dark.

But how does chiaroscuro differ from sfumato? Remember the fog that softened the hard outlines of the figures in Leonardo da Vinci's *Virgin and Child with St. Anne* (page 38)? In chiaroscuro the shadows are darker, the lights are lighter. In other words, the contrasts are greater and sharper.

CARAVAGGIO
The Conversion of St. Paul, about 1601

Does this painting remind you of a stage setting, spotlight and all? This is a perfect example of chiaroscuro.

But first you should know the story the painting tells. On the road to Damascus, a Roman Jew named Saul was suddenly struck down by a great light and was converted to Christianity. Saul then changed his name to Paul and he in turn converted thousands to Christianity.

You can see St. Paul lying on the dark ground, his body thrust diagonally into the painting. His eyes are shut against the blinding light. His hands reach up at the unseen voice. The great light strikes the back of the horse and his uplifted leg, as if St. Paul had just fallen off. His servant tries to pull the horse away. Notice how the strong yellow light dulls the red clothes and cloak of St. Paul. Can you see how the darkness around the light swallows up the edges of the figures, just as it did the edges of the singers at the microphone? Look very closely at the dark shadows in the painting. The dark shadows are not blacks, but are deep reds, browns, and purples.

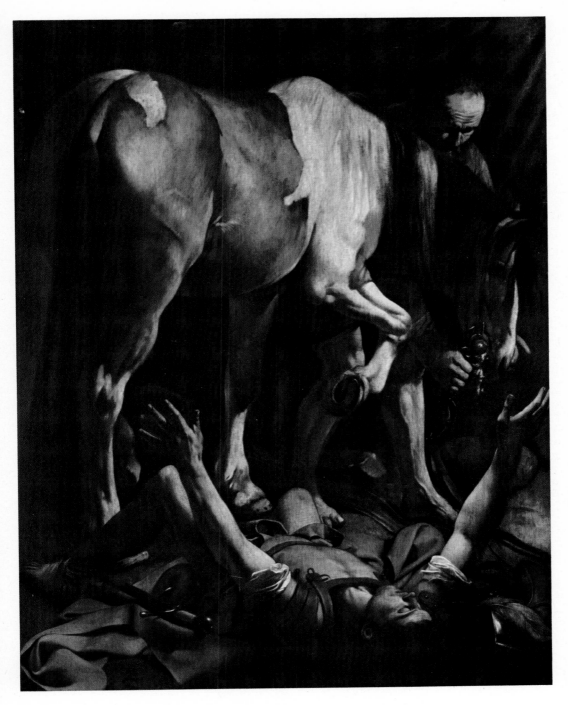

CARAVAGGIO   The Conversion of St. Paul, about 1601. Oil on canvas.
Rome, Santa Maria del Popolo

REMBRANDT VAN RYN
The Anatomy Lesson of Dr. Tulp, 1632

Rembrandt used chiaroscuro to let you see inside the minds of the people he painted. In the *Anatomy Lesson,* Rembrandt chose to paint the moment when Dr. Tulp cut open the arm of the corpse to show his colleagues the muscles and tendons. Look at the faces of the other doctors. Each one reacts differently. The two doctors closest to Dr. Tulp look intensely interested, while the one at the top of the painting looks out at you and points your attention to the scene. But the doctor in the lower left looks away, almost as if he hates to look.

How has Rembrandt used chiaroscuro? As you can see, the outlines of the figures and objects in the room are lost in dark shadows. Light shines only on the corpse, and on the hands, faces, and ruffs of Dr. Tulp and his colleagues. Dr. Tulp's dark clothes also highlight the corpse. Rembrandt has lighted only what he most wants you to see. Look carefully at the luminous colors that shine up through the dark shadows—deep browns, dark reds, greens, and violets. He used his oil paints the way Jan Van Eyck did in *Arnolfini and his Wife* (page 43), laying on thin layers of paint, one on top of the other, to give richness and deeper space to his painting.

REMBRANDT VAN RYN   The Anatomy Lesson of Dr. Tulp, 1632. Oil on canvas. *The Hague, Mauritshuis*

Daylight Is a Cool Light

It is morning. The sun creeps through the open window, touching the desk, the papers, and the pencils and brushes stuck in the china pitcher. The bright sun dances and shimmers on the glass vase filled with dried flowers, and on the ornamented box. But behind each object the sun casts a cool bluish and violet shadow. Around the room, too, where there is light but not sunlight, the white walls are a cool white, faintly tarnished with blues and greens.

Let us say it is now nighttime. The electric light from the lamp falls on the same papers and objects on the desk, casting a yellowish, soft light on everything. But it casts a warm shadow of deep browns and dark reds and purples. Daylight is a cool light (blues and greens and violets), while night light, or artificial light, is warm (yellows, browns, reds, and purples).

JAN VERMEER
Maid Pouring Milk, 1658

You can see sunlight spilling through the cloudy windowpanes, bathing the maid who is pouring milk, and covering the large wall area behind her. The bright sunlight shines on the freshly baked bread in the basket, its crust perhaps crispy and still warm from the oven. The sight of the thin white stream of milk spilling from the pitcher makes one thirsty. One wonders too about what is in the bumpy, blue china pitcher on the table. Even the basket and brass vase hanging in the shadowed corner are gently touched by the sunlight. But the wall under the window is in shadow. It feels cool, like being under a shady tree.

Vermeer has painted thin layers of cool colors, one on top of the other. What are cool colors?—blues, greens, violets, and purples. Now turn back to Rembrandt's *Anatomy Lesson of Dr. Tulp* (page 61) and compare the night light, or artificial light, with Vermeer's daylight. Candlelight or artificial light is yellow, while daylight is white and cool. Rembrandt's shadows are warm deep reds and browns, while Vermeer's shadows are cool blues, greens, and violets. Notice, too, that in painting the maid, he has used cool dark shadows on her right side, in sharp contrast to the sunny yellow wall behind her. But on the left he has let her arm, cap, and dress blend in and become lost with the background.

JAN VERMEER   Maid Pouring Milk, 1658. Oil on canvas. *Amsterdam, Rijksmuseum*

DIEGO VELÁZQUEZ
The Maids of Honor, about 1656

The older maids of honor are coaxing the young Infanta Margarita to return to her parents, the king and queen of Spain. The Infanta had been posing for a family portrait with her parents and had left them.

Do you see the two dwarfs, Maribarbola (on the left) and Nicolasito (on the right, scratching the dog with his foot)? A man, perhaps the tutor, comes into the room through the open doorway in the back. Now look at the mirror on the wall. It reflects King Philip IV of Spain and his queen, who must have been standing just where you are standing now.

In this painting the artist, Velázquez, shows himself at work, painting the portrait of the king and queen. You can see that Velázquez has bathed the Infanta with warm sunlight, because she is the most important person in the painting. The rest of the figures and the room are shadowed in cool colors (blues, greens, and violets). He has used chiaroscuro, spotlighting hands, faces, and places where he wants to take your eye. He lights the edge of the canvas frame, his own hands and face, and the faces of the king and queen in the mirror. He takes you right out through the lighted doorway, but the man coming in brings you back in with him. Your eye comes forward to the tallest maid of honor, the dwarfs, the dog, and back again to the lighted Infanta. Her face is the focal point. Velázquez has also brought the lines of perspective to their vanishing point directly behind her head. And now look at the warmth and softness of the faces, hair, and figures. Wouldn't you like to touch the silky satins, the laces, and the velvets of their clothes?

DIEGO VELÁZQUEZ   The Maids of Honor, about 1656. Oil on canvas.
Madrid, Prado

MEINDERT HOBBEMA
The Avenue at Middelharnis, 1689

This is a painting of daylight, out of doors (a landscape). You feel sun, air, large spaces, and a cloud-strewn sky. The sun shines on the lush green fields, on the road and farm buildings, bathing them in the warm glowing light of late afternoon. The shadows are cool colors. Does this painting remind you of Perugino's painting, *Christ Giving the Keys of the Church to St. Peter* (page 33)? It should, because in both paintings the vanishing point is at the exact center of the horizon line. Follow the lines of the road, the hedgerows, and the trees planted in rows on the right. They all lead *up* to the vanishing point on the horizon line, which is just behind the man walking his dog on the road. The treetops, above the horizon line, come *down* to the vanishing point. Remember, the horizon line is always at the same level as your eyes.

But how does your body make you feel about this painting? Are there somersaults, bouncing rhythms, or zooming diagonals? No, the horizontal lines are like you lying down, while the vertical ones are like you standing still. You are quiet and peaceful when you lie down or when you stand still. And so is this painting by Hobbema quiet and peaceful.

MEINDERT HOBBEMA   The Avenue at Middelharnis, 1689. Oil on canvas.
London, National Gallery

Portraits

A portrait is a painting of a person or a group of persons. Let us say that a photographer takes a series of photographs of you and in each one you have a different expression or look on your face. Which is the *real* you? While you and the photographer have to choose one of the many shots he took of you, a good portrait painter might be able to paint the real you. How? He could paint a combination of many different expressions, giving your face greater depth and showing what you are really like. For instance, he might give a smiling expression to your eyes, but a sad one to your mouth. It is the eyes and mouth in a portrait that give the real likeness and expression to a person's face. But it is the hands, too, particularly the fingers, that often show much about the person's character and characteristics. Of the photographs on the opposite page which one would you have chosen to enlarge?

QUENTIN MASSYS
The Moneylender and His Wife, 1514

Look at the moneylender's long fingers caressing the coins. His wife's fingers are long too, but she is nervously fingering a prayer book. Notice the sharp nose and mouth of the man, the heavy lids on his eyes, so used to picking out valuable coins in the dim light of his room. How sharp the woman's eyes are and how tight her little mouth. See the convex mirror on the table, reflecting the window and building outside. Do you remember where you saw a mirror like it before? (See page 43.) Are the sharp outlines softened by a warm light like that in Leonardo da Vinci's *The Virgin and Child with St. Anne* (page 38). No, the light falling on the faces gives them a roundness and depth, but does not soften them. Even where there are shadows you feel the firm bodies, the folds of their clothes, and the outlines that are always there. Can you see that Massys has surely painted the tools of this man's trade? Money!

QUENTIN MASSYS   The Moneylender and His Wife, 1514. Oil on panel.
Paris, Louvre

LEONARDO DA VINCI
Mona Lisa, about 1504

You can see the softness that seems to surround Mona Lisa. Do you remember this same softness or sfumato in the *Virgin and Child with St. Anne* (page 38)? Do Mona Lisa's eyes and mouth tell you anything? Put your hand over her mouth. Do you think her eyes are smiling? Now move your hand up and cover her eyes—her mouth seems sad. There are two expressions here. It is like putting together two different photographs of one person.

Everyone who looks at the *Mona Lisa* sees something different. Try covering up the entire right side of her face. Her left side looks quite stern, don't you think? Now cover up the left side, and the right side smiles at you, inviting you to love her. What more do *you* see in her face?

Now look at Mona Lisa's hands. They are relaxed, as if she were resigned to sitting there by the open window. Even the fairy landscape behind her adds to the faraway thoughts she seems to be daydreaming about. Leonardo has used bright colors in the foreground, browns and greens in the middle ground, and hazy greens and blues in the faraway background. There are no harsh outlines anywhere; rather a warm, glowing light softens all the lighted areas, while the dark shadows merge gently into each other.

LEONARDO DA VINCI   Mona Lisa, about 1504. Oil on panel. *Paris, Louvre*

DIEGO VELÁZQUEZ
Pope Innocent X, 1650

Do you think this is a portrait of a kindly, lovable, religious man? With your hand, cover up his mouth and look first at his eyes. The steely eyes look deeply and sharply into your soul. They seem almost to have the power to hypnotize. Now cover the eyes and look at the mouth. It seems harsh. In the sixteenth and seventeenth centuries, the Pope was a powerful ruler, who often achieved his ends by the most merciless means. Even his hands with their long fingernails, relaxed as they are, seem to want to reach out for more power and wealth.

Do you remember the detailed richness of silky satins, velvets, and laces in *The Maids of Honor,* also by Velázquez (page 67)? It is all here again plus the gold throne. But notice the way his brush has laid in the long strips of light on the Pope's crimson satin cape and on his lace sleeves and gown. Can you find any harsh outlines here? No, the deep red shadows have swallowed up the edges, while the shadows themselves form interesting shapes. The lighted areas make interesting shapes too.

DIEGO VELÁZQUEZ   Pope Innocent X, 1650. Oil on canvas. *Rome, Doria Pamphili Palace*

FRANS HALS
The Merry Drinker, 1627

What do the eyes and mouth of the Merry Drinker tell you? The twinkling eyes are full of fun, and the mouth seems to sing out a gay song. His left hand holds out his half-filled glass, as if to toast your good health. Look at Hals's way of putting on paint. Does it look the same as the Van Eyck painting on page 43 or the Holbein painting on page 45? Franz Hals put on his paint in a free, loose way, giving you the impression of the whole thing rather than painting tiny details. The broad brushstrokes fairly dance about the canvas. The dashes of paint that model the forms are alive and filled with energy. The lace is done with short fast swirls of white paint, rather than in carefully worked detail. The highlights on the hand are a few fast strokes of paint, while the man's mustache and beard are flicks of brown paint. (You certainly do not see any tiny individual hairs.)

Are there any outlines around the figure? No. Hals has used many of the same colors in the background as in the man's clothes. The Merry Drinker seems to stand out from the background and then mix into it. The only sharp shape is his dark hat and even that merges with the background on the left side. Do you think that Frans Hals himself might have been feeling a bit merry when he painted this portrait?

FRANS HALS   The Merry Drinker, 1627. Oil on canvas. *Amsterdam,*
Rijksmuseum

Reality Versus Make-believe

On the page opposite is an advertisement taken from a fashion magazine. The girl is in a make-believe world of beautiful clothes, perfumes, flowers, and above all, romance. But what if the advertisement had shown a girl dressed in a baggy pair of pajamas, her hair up in curlers, washing her face with soap? You would have turned the page. No one likes to be reminded of what they have to do every day. It is much more fun to dream about a world of fantasy and make-believe.

It was the same during the seventeenth and eighteenth centuries. The world of the ancient Greeks, of gods and goddesses, of poetry and make-believe, was much more desirable than the world of everyday things, or reality. The rich aristocrats did not want to be reminded of the miseries of the poor. They preferred romantic paintings to cover the walls of their châteaus and great houses. Certainly they did not want to be reminded to wash their faces.

Secret of the Sea
The advantage some women have over others

How would it feel to have fresh sea mist delivered to your skin daily? That's the principle of 'Secret of the Sea' cosmetics. Now science has captured the very essence of sea mist in a rare collection of precious complexion creams, lotions, and make-ups.

Take our sea jewels—lipstick and nail enamel that could be melted pearls. A dozen colors, including the new brighter shades of pale. You'll find 'Secret of the Sea' in a secluded beauty harbor, only at superb stores. It's by Dorothy Gray.

SIR JOSHUA REYNOLDS
Garrick between Tragedy and Comedy, about 1761

Reynolds has painted Tragedy and Comedy as if they were two women. He pictures Tragedy as a dreary woman, shrouded in green, with a knife stuck in her belt, obviously voicing all kinds of sad thoughts. Comedy, on the other hand, is pictured as a gay, winsome lass.

David Garrick was a very successful English Shakespearean actor. Can you see the firm grip that Comedy has on his arm? Maybe she is winning the tug-of-war, for Garrick is smiling and moving toward her. He seems to be saying to Tragedy, "Look, Tragedy, you are a lovely, gloomy girl, but Comedy's a lot more fun."

Like Leonardo da Vinci, Sir Joshua Reynolds has bathed the figures in a warm, glowing light, but he has also used chiaroscuro, painting deep shadows that swallow up the outlines of the figures. Can you tell where Garrick's cape begins and the tree trunk ends? Reynolds created two imaginary people to help him paint a great actor of the make-believe world of the stage. But what is that strange mask behind Garrick's shoulder?

SIR JOSHUA REYNOLDS Garrick between Tragedy and Comedy, about 1761. Oil on canvas. *England, Private Collection*

WILLIAM HOGARTH
Marriage à la Mode, scene ii, 1743

There was one British artist, a moralist, who painted people as they really were. Instead of making them beautiful in a make-believe world, he painted them as if they had soap on their faces. In this painting, Hogarth showed a day in the life of an idle, rich nobleman and his lazy wife. The lord, still with his hat on, sits stupidly on a chair while his dog licks the spilled food from his coat. His sword lies broken on the floor—a turned-over chair, a shattered violin, and torn music book nearby. The lord's account-ant, who came to go over the overdrawn accounts, leaves in de-spair, while a servant in the next room wipes his brow trying to clean up the mess. Look at the three pagan gods on and near the mantelpiece. Each is in a niche, garlanded with flowers or candles. It looks as though the lord and lady worship them. They are sym-bolic of what this moralist-artist was trying to say.

There is a feeling of deep space in this painting. If you let your eye follow the reds, it will move in and around the painting. The red footstool and chair focus your eye first on the lord and then on his wife, while the reds in the rug pull your eye to the fallen chair and then into the room beyond. The last touch is the red cord on the chandelier.

Hogarth's painting is like a sermon that scolds the untidy and the lazy.

WILLIAM HOGARTH   Marriage à la Mode, scene ii, 1743. Oil on canvas.
London, National Gallery

JEAN HONORÉ FRAGONARD
The Swing, about 1766

The French court painter Fragonard painted this romantic picture just twenty-three years before the French Revolution. It is a poetic fairyland of trees and flowers and fanciful statues of Cupid and Psyche—Cupid's ladylove—with a lovely girl swinging from a tall tree. As she swings, her lace-trimmed pink dress swirls in billowing folds around her, and her many petticoats tangle about her legs. Can you see her lover hiding in the flowering bush, about to catch the slipper she has flipped into the air? But look behind her. Another lover is swinging her back and forth with a rope. The eternal triangle of love!

Fragonard has bathed the pretty girl in a warm, rosy light, as if the sun had suddenly found its way through the trees. Except for the girl and the moss-covered tree trunk on the right, the rest of the painting, both lights and shadows, has been painted in cool tones, that is, blues and greens. Fragonard has mastered all the skills and techniques of the past to paint textures and light and shadow. He has created a frothy piece of make-believe. Do you wonder that when the starving poor of the French Revolution saw Fragonard's paintings, they cried, "Off with his head!"—and he escaped to Greece just in time?

JEAN HONORÉ FRAGONARD   The Swing, about 1766. Oil on canvas. *London, Wallace Collection*

Violence

This is a picture of violence in the streets today. Students protest and riot over the injustices of segregation and the establishment. Students demand more rights and more say in the running of things. They have now become deeply involved.

After the French Revolution in 1789, most of Europe became involved in war and rebellion. In France, with the king and aristocracy out of the way, the government of the French Republic tottered after its shaky beginning. Napoleon moved in as leader, crowned himself emperor, and began to conquer most of Europe. Now, rich and poor alike became involved in politics, war, and revolution. The artists, too, were involved and used their talents to protest the injustices done or to inspire the people to follow new causes.

It was no longer enough for an artist to paint a pretty girl in a swing.

89

FRANCISCO GOYA
The Third of May, 1808, 1814–15

Like the photograph on the page before, this painting also shows violence. Can you see the French soldiers, faceless in their tall black hats, about to gun down the kneeling man in the white shirt? His arms shoot up in surrender, his voice screams for mercy. But Napoleon's soldiers showed no mercy to the rebelling Spanish citizens of Madrid, during their occupation of Spain. In the next second this man's body will lie next to the other bloody dead. A fresh crowd of victims is pushed from behind into the lighted target area.

Is this chiaroscuro? It certainly is, for Goya has used light and shadow to take your eye where he wants it to go. He has used it like a stage setting. A blinding searchlight drenches the kneeling man and lights up the terrified faces of the next victims. Light falls on the twisted bodies on the ground and glistens on the bayonet points of the aimed rifles. Yellow light blankets the hill behind the man and the ground in front of him, forming a wedge of light. Can you see that half the painting is in light, while the other half is in darkness? The darkness traps the wedge of light, just as the soldiers have trapped their victims and gunned them down.

Are there any small details in this painting? Can you find any textures to touch? No, for Goya has painted with broad, loose brushstrokes, laying in brilliant colors and luminous darks, in large bold areas. Do you remember the loose brushstrokes of Frans Hals's *The Merry Drinker* (page 79)? Goya has made a violent protest against a terrible massacre.

FRANCISCO GOYA   The Third of May, 1808, 1814–15. *Madrid, Prado*

EUGÈNE DELACROIX
Liberty Guiding the People, 1830

"To arms!" shouts Liberty, leading a band of citizens into battle. The purpose of the painting was to stir up the people during the revolution of 1830, which brought Louis Philippe to the throne of France. Do you think this painting is as bloody as Goya's *The Third of May, 1808?*

Just as Reynolds painted Tragedy and Comedy as women (page 83) Delacroix has painted Liberty as a woman racing barefooted and bare-chested across the dead and wounded soldiers, leading the revolutionaries into battle. In her right hand she carries the tricolor, the flag of the French Republic, and in her left a rifle. A young boy with pistols runs beside her. But what about the composition, or road map, of this painting? The sprawled bodies of the dead and wounded carry your eye up to Liberty's right hand holding the flag. In fact, the whole foreground of the painting forms a pyramid, made up of curving shapes, somersaulting curves, and diagonally placed bodies. In the distance you can see the buildings of Paris through the smoke of gunfire. Is this chiaroscuro? You might call it a daytime chiaroscuro, for Delacroix has used the contrasts of light and dark to create a tumultuous and noisy battle scene. Do you think this painting might have helped the cause of the revolution?

EUGÈNE DELACROIX　Liberty Guiding the People, 1830. Oil on canvas.
Paris, Louvre

REALISM AND GUSTAVE COURBET
The Stone Breakers, 1849

Can you tell which is the photograph and which is the painting? On top is the painting of *The Stone Breakers*, which was done in 1849, while on the bottom is a photograph, taken in 1969 (more than one hundred years later) of two workmen tearing down a building. Both camera and artist have caught an unposed moment, as ordinary workmen go about doing their everyday jobs. Do you see that none of the workers looks out at you? In the painting, the stone breaker on the left lifts a heavy basket of crushed stones, while the man on the right hammers on stones lying on the ground. Courbet has given the painting the realistic feeling of a photograph by painting in many small details. He has painted in every detail of the rocks, wooden shoes, striped vest, spoon and lunch pail, scrubby grass, and even the veins on the old man's hands.

The camera was invented just ten years before Courbet painted this picture. It could only take black and white pictures. Do you think it might have influenced Courbet's way of looking at things? This painting has the feeling of black and white, although it actually is painted in subdued colors.

When Courbet began to paint ordinary workingmen the people of Paris were shocked. It never occurred to artists to look about themselves for ideas. But once they did, they found a whole new world to paint. They began to paint the cafés, the people in the park, a girl fresh out of the tub, and even the scrubwomen.

GUSTAVE COURBET   The Stone Breakers, 1849. Oil on canvas. (Destroyed during World War II)

WINSLOW HOMER
Long Branch, New Jersey, 1869

The American painter Winslow Homer looked around at everyday life and found in it much to paint. In this painting two ladies carrying parasols look down to the beach below, leaning into the wind. Do you think the small white dog on the leash might blow away? While this is a realistic everyday beach scene, the painting has a very well worked out composition, or road map. The painting is divided into several large color areas. The jagged shape of green grass carries your eye into the distance. The equally jagged shape of the yellow sandy cliff runs down to the small piece of beach on the left. The blue ocean pulls you across the back of the painting horizontally, while the large shape of the blue sky carries you far off. The details of the painting—the people, the boats, beach, houses, and tiny dog—are fitted into the larger framework of the painting like pieces in a jigsaw puzzle. Even while looking at this ordinary beach scene, Winslow Homer has made you feel the windy cloud-strewn sky, the smell of salt in the air, sand stinging your eyes, and the strong warmth of the sun. Homer has used broad brushstrokes of color, suggesting the impression of details rather than painting them in.

WINSLOW HOMER Long Branch, New Jersey, 1869. Oil on canvas.
Boston, Museum of Fine Arts

ÉDOUARD MANET
The Bar at the Folies Bergères, 1882

The barmaid stands behind the bar staring wistfully at the image that is reflected in the large mirror behind her. Can you see, in the mirror on the right, the image of her back and the man standing in front of her? The man must be standing exactly where you are. (Do you remember the mirror in the painting *The Maids of Honor* by Velázquez, page 67?)

Is this chiaroscuro? No. Why isn't it? There are many lights and darks in this painting, but the darks are not shadows. Look at the man's face in the mirror. His face is a deep color, and there are patches of light on his nose and cheek. Although his face is in shadow, the shadow does not model his face. It is quite flat. It is the same with the barmaid's dress. It is dark blue all over, but it is not shadow. The entire picture is painted with different patches of flat colors—some light, some dark, some bright, some dull. There is almost no modeling with light and dark shadows. These large and small flat patches of color give you the impression of the busy scene, rather than the actual details.

Can you see that the composition is based on a rectangular shape? The girl, her reflection in the mirror, the man, the bar and bottles, are all worked into three large rectangular shapes. Even the front of the girl's dress forms a rectangle.

ÉDOUARD MANET   The Bar at the Folies Bergères, 1882. Oil on canvas.
London, Courtauld Institute Galleries

EDGAR DEGAS
The Absinthe Drinker, 1876

Edgar Degas also painted an everyday café scene. But there is no gaiety reflected in the mirror behind—only the two blurred and dark shapes of the sad girl and the man in the black hat. Why did Degas paint the couple so far over to the right, with the man partly out of the painting? Degas wanted to show you the sadness of the absinthe drinkers and he used techniques of composition to do it. The flat, empty tables in the left foreground give a feel of loneliness. By painting the man half out of the picture, Degas cuts him off from the girl who stares sadly into her glass of yellow absinthe, making her seem even lonelier than ever.

Why isn't your eye carried out of the picture with the man? Degas has divided the painting into big sections: the three white tables, the floor, the brown bench, and the mirror behind. The two sitting figures tie these big areas together, holding you in the painting.

Are the figures modeled with light and shadow? No. Just as in Manet's painting of the bar at the Folies Bergères, there are large areas or patches of light and dark colors. Nevertheless, the figures look very solid. (Degas often modeled figures in clay.) There is something else too. The paint itself has a shimmer and lightness. Brushstrokes of color dance across the surface of the painting, giving it a new excitement. With a fresh use of composition and color, Degas has caught the impression of a single, fleeting moment in the lonely lives of two people.

EDGAR DEGAS   The Absinthe Drinker, 1876. Oil on canvas. *Paris, Musée de l'Impressionnisme*

How Do You Paint Sunlight?

Sunlight striking black wool is absorbed. Sunlight striking snow reflects back a blinding white glare. Sunlight striking rain makes a rainbow of colors. But sunlight striking water mirrors itself in the ripples.

The photograph on the opposite page was taken from a bridge high above a big river. The river currents and windswept waves catch and mirror the sunrays in a pattern of tiny particles of light. There is a small dark pool on the left, where the wind and waves have not stirred the water. Notice that the sun has mirrored itself in several little shimmering stars?

How does an artist paint this shimmer and sparkle of light that are never still for even a moment?

CLAUDE MONET
Water Lilies, Midday, 1918

Claude Monet painted sunlight sparkling on water. The light leaps and dances on the water's surface, reflecting the sun, patches of open sky, and the trees and bushes close by. Here and there the muddy water shows through from underneath. And sailing on the surface like small boats are white water lilies. Green lily pads float just below the surface, showing their own green wetness.

How did Monet paint this picture of sunlight on the pond? When you first look at this painting you feel its greenness. However, if you look closely, you will see that the painting is made up of many different colors—pale violets, deep purples, blues, lemon yellows, dark reds, pinks, and also olive greens, yellow greens, and blue greens. Each color is a separate brushstroke. Monet has laid on fast swirling brushstrokes of paint that catch the never-ending movement and shimmer of sunlight. Stand away from the picture. Can you see that your eye mixes the many separate colors, leaving you with a shimmering and sparkling greenness? But is this painting just a disorganized maze of colors? No. If you squint at the painting you can see the carefully planned composition, or road map, that carries your eye in and around the picture.

CLAUDE MONET Water Lilies, Midday, 1918. Oil on canvas. *Zürich,*
Bührle Collection

PIERRE AUGUSTE RENOIR
Bather Drying Herself, 1910

Renoir painted this lovely bather with as rosy a skin as Peter Paul Rubens painted his sea nymphs in *The Landing of Maria de' Medici* (page 55). But the sea nymphs were creatures of mythology, while Renoir painted a scene from his own everyday life. Yellow and green trees and bushes fill in the background space, while sun and air give a shimmer and translucent quality to the bather's rosy body. Can you find any deep shadows? Are there any large flat areas, as in Manet's painting of *The Bar at the Folies Bergères?* There are none of those here. Renoir has modeled a round, solid girl, as if with clay, but instead of using light and dark to model her, he has used warm and cold colors. He used warm rosy reds, pinks, yellows, and pastel or light oranges to pull the forms out toward you. He used cool violets, greens, and blues to push the forms back into the picture. For example, look at the way in which he has painted the folds of the white towel. The ridges of the folds are pink, while the creases are blue and purple. Renoir painted with small, soft brushfuls of different pastel (light) colors. Just as Monet did, he lets your eye blend these colors together at a distance. But why does the skin of the girl seem so luminous and warm? Did you know that when you put a warm color next to a cool color the warm color looks warmer, and the cool color looks cooler? Do you think the cool blues and greens of the background help make the girl's skin seem even rosier?

PIERRE AUGUSTE RENOIR Bather Drying Herself, about 1910. Oil on
canvas. *São Paulo, Museum and Art Gallery*

Blowup

Look closely at this blown-up photograph of a college student. Can you see the separate dots that make up the black, white, and gray areas? When the photograph is reduced in size, these tiny dots merge together to make a solid gray, or black, area. It is also true that if you stand far away from the picture, your eye will merge and mix the tiny dots into a solid area. It is this use of the human eye to mix small dots of color that fascinated Georges Seurat.

GEORGES SEURAT
A Sunday Afternoon on the Island of La Grande Jatte, 1885

Seurat carries your eye far into space in this painting of a lazy Sunday afternoon in the park. The figures and trees grow slowly smaller and less clear as they move back to the vanishing point. The vanishing point is behind the heads of the two strolling figures in the foreground. There is so much going on. Can you see the man tooting on his horn, the little girl skipping, the many boats on the lake, the black dog sniffing the lady's sandwich, and the monkey on the leash?

Do you think that the figures look as if they had been modeled out of wet sand? If you look closely, you can see that Seurat painted with thousands of tiny dots of different colors of paint. This new method that he invented was called pointillism. Do the dots remind you of the enlarged photograph on the previous page? Instead of mixing yellow and blue to make green, Seurat placed tiny dots of blue and yellow next to each other. It is the eye that mixes them. To make dark green, Seurat used more dark blue dots than yellow. Sometimes he added tiny dots of opposite colors, or complementary colors. (If you put a red next to a green, the green looks greener and the red looks redder. It is the same with blue and orange, and yellow and purple.) Seurat carefully built his painting out of thousands of tiny grains of colored paint, and it is these small dots that give his paintings such a shimmer of light and air.

GEORGES SEURAT   A Sunday Afternoon on the Island of La Grande Jatte,
1885. Oil on canvas. *Chicago, Art Institute, Helen Birch Bartlett Memorial Collection*

VINCENT VAN GOGH
Starry Night, 1889

There is excitement and mystery here. Van Gogh has painted this starry night as if the stars and moon were whirling around in their orbits, leaving behind a fiery path of light. The wind seems to somersault across the dark sky, while the moon lights up its tumblings. Even the trees leap flamelike into the sky. The village, too, seems to possess its own inner life and energy. Here and there a roof, a window, an open door, or church steeple give off an eerie light.

While Seurat used paint as if it were different colored grains of sand, to build his rounded forms, Van Gogh used his brush-strokes of color as if they had an energy in themselves. They somersault and dance across the painting. Van Gogh began with a strong outline, drawing in the objects in bright or dark colors. This outline gave things their own shape and character. Then he took brushfuls of color and repeated the shape over and over in a brilliance of many colors. For example, look at the dark green out-line around the hills. Inside each hill the colors repeat its shape over and over. While Van Gogh left it to the eye to mix the colors, he excited the mind with his violent movement. Each object seems to have a life of its own. It is as if he saw something in nature that we cannot see. Or do you see it too?

VINCENT VAN GOGH   Starry Night, 1889. Oil on canvas. *New York, Museum of Modern Art, Lillie P. Bliss Bequest*

HENRI DE TOULOUSE-LAUTREC
Au Cirque Fernando, 1888

The circus horse ridden by the pretty lady acrobat gallops around the circus ring, directed by the ringmaster. Can you see that most of the spectators and the clown are half out of the painting? The painting really tells the story of the cruel ringmaster, the fearful girl, and the wary horse. Both the girl and the horse look backward, eyeing the ringmaster. His face looks mean and arrogant as he slashes about their legs with his long whip.

How does Toulouse-Lautrec use his paint? Are there small brushstrokes of color, dots, or exciting slashes of color? Toulouse-Lautrec has drawn his figures with line and filled them in with color. But the lines are not just outlines. They are full of life, sometimes thick and bold, sometimes fine, then disappearing completely. But always the line describes the form, action, and personality. The color areas are soft and sketchy, as if he had merely laid in large areas of paint, planning to put in more detail later on.

What keeps your eye from galloping out of the painting with the horse? The invisible lines of hate between the ringmaster, the girl, and the horse hold your eye in the center. Toulouse-Lautrec delighted in painting dancers and performers in the cafés as well as in the circus. He painted lecherous men, hatcheck girls, and barmaids too, catching with his brush their greedy smiles, their put-on gaiety, or their loneliness.

HENRI DE TOULOUSE-LAUTREC   Au Cirque Fernando, 1888. Oil on canvas. *Chicago, Art Institute*

PAUL GAUGUIN
Women of Tahiti, 1891

When Paul Gauguin turned thirty-five, he gave up his job as a stockbroker in a Paris bank and began to paint. At the age of fifty-three he sailed for Tahiti, where he painted many wonderful pictures. He was a religious man, and many of the women he painted had a Madonnalike quality. The girl in pink seems lost in deep thought. She fingers an orange vine, making circular patterns with it on the sand, as if it spelled out some special meaning. The girl on the left sits with her eyes closed, as if listening to an inner voice. She leans on her strong right arm. It is as thick and powerful as the arms of Michelangelo's Delphic Sibyl (page 51). But here the powerful arm seems to mean strong religious belief rather than strong pent-up energy. The girl's red skirt forms a large, flat, red shape, enclosed by an outline broken only by the pattern of white flowers. An outline also encloses the solid girl in pink, sitting cross-legged, cutting her off from her companion. But she is very peaceful.

Behind, the dark green sea washes quietly on the beach. Look at the sandy spaces surrounding the two figures. They make interesting shapes. Gauguin seems to have built his painting with large, beautifully colored shapes. He has used little shadow to model his figures; instead, he has used deeper, or more brilliant, colors, or again, simply a line, to suggest rounded forms. Just as Michelangelo let the Delphic Sibyl burst out of her niche, so does Gauguin let his two women burst out of the picture frame.

PAUL GAUGUIN   Women of Tahiti, 1891. Oil on canvas. *Paris, Musée de l'Impressionnisme*

House of Cards

This is a photograph of a house of cards. The house is built up by placing cards at an angle, one on top of or behind the other. Imagine that each card is a different color. An orange card would come forward, while a blue one would recede into the background. In other words, the warm color comes forward and the cool color goes back.

Cézanne saw the world in colored planes or as a colored house of cards. He looked at a hill and translated it into cards or flat planes of color, building it up carefully, letting a warm plane be next to a cool plane. This gives the hill a pull and a push in and out of space. If he had built with building blocks he could not have done it with more care or planning. The result gives the painting a strong sense of structure and a deep feeling of color harmony.

When you look at nature, or the world around you, do you see it as a house of cards?

PAUL CÉZANNE
Mont Sainte-Victoire, about 1906

Follow the large areas of orange from the foreground to the background. They lead you like stepping-stones back to the blue mountain which is the focal point. Now do the same with the dark greens. Can you see that the whole picture is made up of small planes or flat cards of color? A warm yellow-green plane is placed next to a cool blue-green plane—a red one next to a greenish one. Look at the pale-yellow, red, and orange planes on the orange hill in the left foreground. Some of them form fields and rooftops and walls of houses. Can you see to its right, the houses nestled in the green valley?

The blue mountain rises in the distance, blending its flat blue-green color planes with those of the sky. A strong line, here and there, separates the two areas. The warm planes come toward you, while the cool planes recede. Can you feel the pull and push in and out of space of all these planes? By squinting, you can also see that Cézanne has repeated the shape of the mountain in the landscape, over and over, accenting its shape.

Does Cézanne's use of color remind you of Monet or Seurat? Cézanne built forms the way an architect builds a house, board on top of board, plane on top of plane. It usually took him years to complete a single painting to its perfection of harmony and color.

PAUL CÉZANNE   Mont Sainte-Victoire, about 1906. Oil on canvas. *Philadelphia, Museum of Art, collection George W. Elkins*

In Conclusion

Cézanne saw the world as a house of colored cards, and later painters were fascinated by his building ability. If Cézanne could build a world of forms with colored cards or planes, they reasoned, why then couldn't they break it down, scatter the cards in all directions, and rebuild the world in their own eyes? This experimentation with color planes, forms, and shapes was the beginning of modern art. And it was Cézanne who began it all.

Now that you have looked at hundreds of years of paintings and painters, how does your world look to you? Are you able to see any new things around you that you never noticed before? When you see a plump policeman on his horse, does he remind you of Martini's Guidoriccio, riding around his castle on his horse, or of Uccello's St. George on his wooden-looking horse? When you see a grieving woman, do you remember Mary weeping in Giotto's *Lamentation over Christ* or the sad woman in Degas's *Absinthe Drinker?* When you see violence at night, do you think of *The Conversion of St. Paul*, by Caravaggio, or *The Third of May, 1808*, by Goya?

If by looking carefully at paintings you have learned to see fresh new things in the cracks of the sidewalk, or new patterns in the branches of a tree, then this book has achieved its purpose. Whether you are looking at paintings or life around you, your eyes should always be wide open.

DATES	SOME MAJOR DATES IN WORLD HISTORY	ARTIST OR PAINTING INCLUDED
3110–1198 B.C.	Rule of first to nineteenth dynasties in Egypt	*Fowling in the Marshes* (Egyptian painting)
973–933 B.C.	Reign of King Solomon of Israel	
753 B.C.	Romulus and Remus found Rome	
550–529 B.C.	Reign of Cyrus the Great, founder of Persian Empire	Greek Vase: "Harnessing a Chariot"
459 B.C.	Pericles, leader of Athens—First Peloponnesian War	
334–331 B.C.	Alexander the Great conquers Persian Empire	
218 B.C.	Hannibal crosses the Alps—defeats Roman armies	
101–44 B.C.	Julius Caesar	
8–4 B.C.	Jesus of Nazareth born	
A.D. 29	Jesus is crucified	
117–138	Reign of Hadrian, Roman emperor	
312	Emperor Constantine converts to Christianity	
410	Goths sack Rome	
527–565	Reign of Justinian I, Byzantine emperor	Byzantine Empress *Theodora and Her Courtiers*
768–814	Reign of Charlemagne	
1066	William I, called William the Conqueror; Normans defeat Saxons at the Battle of Hastings	
1095	First Crusade to the Holy Land by French and Normans	
1189	Richard the Lion-Hearted—Third Crusade	
1215	King John of England signs Magna Charta	Cimabue (Italian) 1240–1302 GOTHIC
1271–95	Marco Polo travels to China	Giotto (Italian) 1276?–?1337 EARLY RENAISSANCE

DATES	SOME MAJOR DATES IN WORLD HISTORY	ARTIST OR PAINTING INCLUDED
1337–1453	Hundred Years' War between France and England	
1347–50	Black Death epidemic of the plague in Europe	Simone Martini (Italian) 1283?–1344 INTERNATIONAL GOTHIC
1431	Joan of Arc burned at the stake at Rouen	
1453	Fall of Constantinople; end of Byzantine Empire	Limbourg Brothers (French) c.1415 INTERNATIONAL GOTHIC Uccello (Italian) 1396–1475 EARLY RENAISSANCE
1458	Johann Gutenberg of Germany prints first Bible (invented printing with movable type).	Jan Van Eyck (Flemish) 1370?–?1440 EARLY RENAISSANCE
1471–84	Papacy of Sixtus IV, patron of the Renaissance; builds Sistine Chapel at Vatican	Perugino (Italian) 1446–1523 EARLY RENAISSANCE
1478–92	Rule of Lorenzo de' Medici (the Magnificent) of Florence	
1492	Columbus discovers America	Raphael (Italian) 1483–1520
1509–47	Reign of Henry VIII of England	
1513	Spanish explorer Balboa discovers the Pacific	HIGH RENAISSANCE Massys (Flemish) 1466?–1530
1517	Protestant Reformation in Germany —Martin Luther	NORTHERN RENAISSANCE Leonardo da Vinci (Italian) 1452–1519
1529	Sir Thomas More becomes chancellor of England	HIGH RENAISSANCE Michelangelo (Italian) 1475–1564
1556–98	Spanish Inquisition under Philip II	HIGH RENAISSANCE

DATES	SOME MAJOR DATES IN WORLD HISTORY	ARTIST OR PAINTING INCLUDED
1558–1603	Reign of Queen Elizabeth I of England	Holbein the Younger (German) 1497?–1543 NORTHERN RENAISSANCE Bruegel the Elder (Flemish) 1520?–69 NORTHERN RENAISSANCE
1588	Defeat of Spanish Armada by English	El Greco (Spanish) 1548?–?1614 RENAISSANCE
1607	Captain James Smith founds Jamestown, Virginia	Caravaggio (Italian) 1573–1610 BAROQUE
1611–48	Thirty Years' War between Catholics and Protestants on Continent and in England	Rubens (Flemish) 1577–1640 BAROQUE Rembrandt (Dutch) 1606–69 BAROQUE
1620	Pilgrims land at Plymouth Rock, Massachusetts	Frans Hals (Dutch) 1580?–1666 BAROQUE
1648	Independence of Dutch Republic	
1643–1715	Reign of Louis XIV (the Sun King) of France	
1689–1702	Reign of William and Mary in England	Velázquez (Spanish) 1599–1660 BAROQUE
1702–63	Series of colonial wars between England and France	Vermeer (Dutch) 1632–75 BAROQUE
1713–40	Reign of Frederick William I of Prussia (first king)	Hobbema (Dutch) 1638–1709 BAROQUE
1715–74	Reign of Louis XV of France	Hogarth (English) 1697–1764 BAROQUE
1760–1820	King George III of England rules	
1773	Boston Tea Party	Reynolds (English) 1723–92
1775–83	American War for Independence	
1776	Declaration of Independence	
1789–99	French Revolution	Fragonard (French) 1732–1806 ROCOCO

DATES	SOME MAJOR DATES IN WORLD HISTORY	ARTIST OR PAINTING INCLUDED
1793–94	Reign of Terror; execution of Louis XVI and Marie Antoinette	
1796–1815	Napoleonic Wars	Goya (Spanish) 1746–1828 ROMANTICISM
1804–14	Reign of Napoleon; crowns himself emperor	
1812–14	War of 1812 between United States and England	
1815	Battle of Waterloo; Napoleon exiled	
1830	July revolution; Louis Philippe becomes constitutional monarch. Abdication of French King Charles X	Delacroix (French) 1798–1863 ROMANTICISM
1836	Battle of the Alamo, Texas	
1837–1901	Reign of Queen Victoria in England	Courbet (French) 1819–77 REALISM
1848	Revolutions in Hungary, Prussia, Austria, France, etc.	
1852–70	Reign of Napoleon III, emperor of France	Manet (French) 1832–83 IMPRESSIONISM
1854–56	Crimean War; Great Britain, France against Russia	
1861–65	American Civil War	Homer (American) 1836–1910 REALISM
1870–71	Franco-Prussian War; France surrenders	Degas (French) 1834–1917 IMPRESSIONISM
1871	Paris Commune	
1871	Bismarck and the unification of the German Empire	Monet (French) 1840–1926 IMPRESSIONISM
1888–1918	Kaiser William II rules Germany; pushes out Bismarck	
1898	Spanish-American War; USS *Maine* explodes in harbor of Havana	Renoir (French) 1841–1919 IMPRESSIONISM

DATES	SOME MAJOR DATES IN WORLD HISTORY	ARTIST OR PAINTING INCLUDED
1914	Panama Canal opened	Van Gogh (Dutch) 1853–90 POST-IMPRESSIONISM
1914	Assassination of Archduke Ferdinand, heir to Austrian throne	Seurat (French) 1859–91 POST-IMPRESSIONISM
1914–18	World War I	Toulouse-Lautrec (French) 1864–1901 REALISM
1917	Russian revolution	
1919	Treaty of Versailles	Gauguin (French) 1848–1903 POST-IMPRESSIONISM Cézanne (French) 1839–1906 IMPRESSIONISM

About the Artists

BRUEGEL (*brur*-ghel)   1525?–1569

Pieter Bruegel the Elder, so called because he had two sons who were also very fine painters, was born in a small village in the Netherlands. He is most famous for his huge paintings full of action and movement that show in marvelous detail the lives of the peasants of his country.

CARAVAGGIO (*ka*-ra-*vad*-jo)   1573–1609

After studying painting in Milan, Michelangelo da Caravaggio moved to Rome. He lived a wild and violent life and was always in trouble with officials of the church and state. His paintings are very dramatic and full of light and shadow. He used many poor and ordinary people as models for his pictures of great saints.

CÉZANNE (*say-zan*)   1839–1906

Paul Cézanne was born in southern France. His father wanted him to be a lawyer, but the young man was far more interested in becoming a painter. When he was twenty-two years old he went to Paris to study art. There he met many famous painters who were working in a new style called impressionism. Their paintings were full of color and light; instead of trying to make their paintings look like photographs, they painted their own impression of the way things looked. Cézanne's entire life was dedicated to painting. He has been called the greatest innovator of art in the nineteenth century.

CIMABUE (*chee*-mah-*boo*-uh)   c.1240–c.1302

Giovanni Cimabue, who lived most of his life in Florence, Italy, was most famous for starting a new way of painting people and their faces. He tried to make them look natural and lifelike. He taught many young painters. His most famous pupil was Giotto.

COURBET (koor-*bay*)   1819–1877

Gustave Courbet, a French painter who learned to paint by copying great masterpieces, was the founder of a school of painting called realism. He lived and worked most of his life in Paris. Courbet took an active and often unpopular position in many political issues and finally had to flee to Switzerland for safety.

DA VINCI, LEONARDO (lay-o-*nard*-o da *veen*-chi)   1452–1519

Leonardo was brought up in Florence, Italy. He was perhaps the most gifted of all the artists who lived at the time of the Renaissance. He was an artist who worked in any medium, an architect, and an engineer. His fresco *Last Supper* and his portrait *Mona Lisa* are among the best-known works of art in all history. Among his thousands of drawings are plans for airplanes and many other complicated machines that are taken for granted today as part of our lives.

DEGAS (d'-*ga*)   1834–1917

Edgar Degas was born in Paris. He was one of a group called the impressionists. Having plenty of money, he did not have to sell his paintings; he liked to keep them in his studio where he could make little changes whenever he wanted to. His style was free and daring and he worked in both oils and pastels. Many of his most famous works portray ballerinas and dancing girls. As he grew older he began to avoid his friends, spending most of his time alone. At the age of eighty-three, almost blind, he committed suicide.

DELACROIX (del-la-*crwa*)   1798–1863

Eugène Delacroix was known as the leader of the romantic movement in French painting. He was born near Paris, but traveled a great deal in North Africa, and his paintings are famous for their hot, vivid colors. The murals that he painted for the walls of several Paris libraries and public buildings are as remarkable as his paintings.

FRAGONARD (fra-gon-*ar*)   1732–1806

Jean Honoré Fragonard was still a young man when he came to Paris from his home in southern France to study art. His delicate, colorful paintings greatly impressed the French nobility. For many years his beautifully detailed scenes of love and gallantry made him a favorite of the court of Louis XVI.

GAUGUIN (go-*gan*) 1848–1903

Paul Gauguin was born in Paris. He became a sailor and later a successful banker. Painting had been his hobby for many years, but when he was thirty-five he decided he must devote all of his time to painting. During the years that followed, he tried to support his wife and children but his paintings were unpopular and unsalable. He loved the sea and tropical countries and in 1891 he left France to live and paint in Tahiti. In 1893 he came back to France but later returned to the South Pacific islands and to the people and the only way of life he could endure.

GIOTTO (gi-*ot*-to) 1276?–1337?

Giotto di Bondone, famous Florentine painter, may have had more influence on the development of art in Europe than any other artist. His paintings are natural and lifelike. His students, to whom he was both teacher and hero, were important members of the artistic movement called the Renaissance.

GOYA (*go*-ya) 1746–1828

Francisco de Goya y Lucientes, born in a small, poor village in Spain, began to draw when he was very young. After years of study with various teachers he settled in Madrid. He became court painter to the king of Spain and painted many portraits of nobles and their children in glorious, glowing colors. During the occupation of Spain by Napoleon, Goya produced a series of drawings and etchings on the horrors of war that have never been surpassed.

GRECO, EL (el *gray*-ko) 1548?–?1614

This great painter, who was called the Greek, was born in Crete. He studied art in Venice, Italy, and later settled in Toledo, Spain, where he lived the rest of his life. His style is very personal and is made very dramatic by flamelike colors and great contrasts.

HALS (*hols*) 1580?–1666

Frans Hals was born in Antwerp and spent most of his life in Haarlem, the center of art and painting in Holland. He produced many portraits—both of individuals and groups—that are considered second only to the work of the immortal Rembrandt.

HOBBEMA (*hobb*-em-a)   1638–1709
Meindert Hobbema, one of Holland's foremost landscapists, was born in Amsterdam. He is best known for his paintings of woodlands, farmhouses, and water mills in the countryside surrounding him. Almost all of his paintings were executed before 1689; many of these paintings are in England, where they have influenced later landscape artists. Hobbema is said to have studied under Jakob van Ruisdael.

HOGARTH (*ho*-garth)   1697–1764
William Hogarth was born in London. He was the son of a schooolteacher. Hogarth started drawing when he was a child and learned the art of engraving on silver and copper while still a teen-ager. He is best known for several series of prints that he engraved and printed himself. His most famous drawings were satirical comments on the life and the people he saw around him.

HOLBEIN (*hol*-bine)   1497?–1543
Hans Holbein, called "the younger" because his father had the same name and was an artist, too, was born in Germany. An artist of many different talents, he illustrated books, painted portraits, and decorated buildings. He visited many countries and became friends with many famous people of his time. He finally settled in England, where he died, one of the few artists to enjoy fame and fortune during his own lifetime.

HOMER (*ho*-mer)   1836–1910
Winslow Homer was born in Boston. He worked as a war correspondent during the Civil War, and his pictures of Negro life after the war made him internationally famous. His greatest talent was his genius for painting watercolor interpretations of the sea.

DE LIMBOURG (de *lim*-boorg)   Early 15th Century
The three de Limbourg brothers, Pol, Jean, and Hermann, were born in the Netherlands. They were apprenticed to a goldsmith in Paris. Pol was employed by the duke of Burgundy for part of his lifetime. The three brothers worked on one famous painting together for many years. The painting was still unfinished at the time of their deaths.

MANET (ma-*nay*)   1832–1883
Édouard Manet was born in Paris. He was the son of a wealthy lawyer. At

the age of sixteen he joined the navy but soon resigned to study art. He became one of the most respected and admired of the group of painters known as the impressionists. His fresh and original approach to painting made younger painters look up to him as a master, but he was denied approval and recognition by critics and the public until shortly before his death.

MARTINI (mar-*ti*-ni) 1283?–1344
Simone Martini was an Italian artist who was most famous for the frescoes he created for Italian churches and chapels. Fresco (*fress*-coe) is a way of painting on damp, fresh plaster.

MASSYS (mass-*ice*) 1466?–1530
Quentin Massys was Flemish, the son of a locksmith. He first worked as a blacksmith and then went to Antwerp to study art. He lived and worked during a time when the impact of the Italian Renaissance was beginning to be felt in northern Europe, and the rich, glowing colors of his paintings reflect this influence.

MICHELANGELO (*my*-kel-*an*-gelo) 1475–1564
Michelangelo Buonarroti, Italian sculptor, architect, poet, and painter, was the supreme artist of the sixteenth century. His lovely statue *Pietà*, completed when he was twenty-five years old, established him as the outstanding sculptor of his time. The almost unbelievable beauty of the Sistine Chapel ceiling, in addition to his other artistic achievements, has aroused the wonder and respect of the world for over four hundred years.

MONET (mo-*nay*) 1840–1926
Claude Monet was the son of a French grocer. While still young he dedicated himself to painting. After studying in Paris he became associated with the impressionist school of painting. He was primarily interested in landscapes and often painted the same field over and over again, showing how the changing light affected the way it looked. He was almost blind for the last ten years of his life, but he lived to enjoy the acclaim and success that his work deserved.

PERUGINO (pair-u-*gi*-no)   1446–1523

Pietro Vannucci, called Il Perugino, was born near Perugia, Italy. As a result of much study and practice, his work became well known, and he was invited to paint several frescoes for the Sistine Chapel. Some of these later were removed to make way for the *Last Judgment* by Michelangelo.

RAPHAEL (ra-pha-*el*)   1483–1520

Raphael was the son of a local painter in Urbino, Italy. By the time he was seventeen years old his work was considered superior to that of the masters under whom he was studying. When he moved to Florence he came under the influence of Michelangelo and Leonardo da Vinci. He died when he was thirty-seven, but in twenty years he created a body of work that places him among the very greatest painters of history.

REMBRANDT (*rem*-brant)   1606–1669

Rembrandt was the son of a prosperous miller of Leiden, Holland. He adopted the surname van Rijn, which means "of the Rhine." He first began to study literature, but his real talent was drawing. After having been apprenticed to several painters, he returned to Leiden. As his genius flowered, so did his domestic troubles and debts. His magnificent technique and the great humanity revealed in his work made his portraits and portrait groups much sought after. Money troubles haunted him all his life but his influence was immense in his own day and has never faded.

RENOIR (ren-*wa*)   1841–1919

Pierre Auguste Renoir was born in Limoges, France. When he was thirteen he went to work in a ceramics factory. His talent for drawing soon became apparent, and when he had saved enough money he went to Paris to take up the serious study of art. He became friends with the impressionist group, and his paintings of the people and pleasures of ordinary life were well received. In his later years his talent reached its height and he exhibited often and with great success and acclaim.

REYNOLDS (*ren*-olds)   1723–1792

Joshua Reynolds was born in the county of Devon, England. His father had been a member of the faculty of Oxford University and at the time of

Joshua's birth was head of the local grammar school. Joshua decided early upon a career as a painter. He studied in London and then in all the great centers of painting in Europe. Upon his return he soon became the most sought-after portrait painter in England. He was knighted in 1769.

RUBENS (*roo*-benz)   1577–1640
Peter Paul Rubens was born in Germany, where his father was in exile from his native Holland. After his father's death the youthful Rubens and his family moved to Antwerp, where he attended a Jesuit school, became a court page, learned several languages, and began his career as a painter. He spent nine years in Italy before returning to Antwerp, where he very quickly became famous. The marvelous coloring and movement of his pictures created so much demand for his work that he hired young artists to do the basic drawing. He then finished the works in his own style.

SEURAT (su-*rah*)   1859–1891
Georges Seurat was born in Paris and was identified with the city and its art world during all of his short life. He developed an original theory of painting called pointillism. In this technique, colors are not mixed by the painter. Pure color is applied in tiny dots and the resulting blend is made by the eye of the viewer.

TOULOUSE-LAUTREC (too-*loos*-lo-*trek*)   1864–1901
Henri de Toulouse-Lautrec was the son of a French nobleman. He broke both legs when he was a child and as a result was permanently deformed. He did most of his schoolwork at home. When he was eighteen he decided to study painting only. At the age of twenty he moved into his own studio in Paris. He loved Paris night life and all the different kinds of people that lived it and enjoyed it. He made no distinction between "pure" art and "commercial" art. In addition to painting portraits and landscapes, he designed posters, menus, and theater programs.

UCCELLO (oo-*chel*-lo)   1397–1475
Paolo Uccello was born in Florence, Italy. Uccello was not his real name, but a nickname given him because of his love of birds (*uccello* means "bird"

in Italian). He was apprenticed to one of the greatest sculptors of his time, but turned to painting as his lifework. He was called a realist, and is best known for his series of paintings of the Battle of San Romano.

VAN EYCK   (van *ike*)   1370?–1441
Jan van Eyck was a painter about whose early life little is known. In 1422 he became painter to John, duke of Holland. During the last ten years of his life he produced his greatest paintings, noted for their remarkable brilliance of color.

VAN GOGH   (van *goh*)   1853–1890
Vincent van Gogh was born in the Dutch province of Brabant. As a youth he felt that preaching the Word of God should be his lifework. But he began to draw, and when he was twenty-seven years old he dedicated his future to art. When he went to Paris and saw the work of the impressionists his whole somber style of painting changed. His canvases began to explode with bright, powerful color. He moved to the south of France, where Gauguin lived with him for brief periods. Vincent began to have periods of great depression that deepened into severe mental illness. In 1890 he committed suicide.

VELÁZQUEZ   (vay-*la*-sketh)   1599–1660
Diego Velazquez was born in Seville, Spain. He began to study painting before he was twelve years old, and all his life he approached his work as a student striving for perfection. He traveled widely and knew and observed the works of most of the famous painters of his time. When Diego and his family moved to Madrid in 1623, he became the favorite court painter and an intimate friend of King Philip IV's.

VERMEER   (ver-*mare*)   1632–1675
Jan Vermeer was born in Delft, Holland, and apparently spent his whole life there. He did not enjoy recognition or fame during his lifetime, but today is regarded as one of the greatest Dutch masters and one of the world's finest colorists. His favorite scenes were interiors, with single figures exquisitely detailed and beautifully lifelike.

Index